50 Ways to Celebrate Life After 50

Get unstuck, avoid regrets and live your best life!

Suzy Rosenstein MA

Master Life Coach & Midlife Mentor
Host of Women in the Middle® Podcast

Suzy Rosenstein
info@suzyrosenstein.com

50 Ways to Celebrate Life after 50: Get unstuck, avoid regrets and live your best life/ Suzy Rosenstein. —1st ed.

Paperback ISBN: 978-1-7774801-0-3
Hardcover ISBN: 978-1-7774801-2-7
eBook ISBN: 978-1-7774801-1-0

*To my three loving parents who raised me and each contributed
to my ability to overcome adversity, see the glass as half-full
and become the woman I am today.*

Praise for
50 Ways to Celebrate Life After 50

· ·

Get excited about being 50+! It's the BEST time for a woman to live in her power. 50 Ways to Celebrate Life After 50 is your guide to celebrating your feminine pleasure, wisdom, talent, beauty and sexuality.

SUSAN HYATT, BEST SELLING AUTHOR OF BARE

Who knew life beyond 50 could actually be great? 50 Ways to Celebrate Life after 50 is a book I wish I had as I turned the mid-century mark! If you are turning 50 soon or have left 50 in the dust, it's not too early or too late for a real reboot. I used to think that getting older meant having to settle for less. Less fun, less satisfaction with myself and with life as a whole. But this book shows you how to blast through those old-school beliefs and get the absolute MOST out of every day going forward. Make time for yourself and make time to dive into this little but powerful book. You're welcome.

COOKIE ROSENBLUM, AUTHOR, CLEARING YOUR PATH TO PERMANENT WEIGHT LOSS, HOST OF THE WEIGHT LOSS MADE REAL PODCAST

Stressed about getting older? Worried that your best years are behind you? This is the book for you! With love, humor and a lot of straight talk, Suzy Rosenstein has created a guide to change your perspective so you can not just enjoy your post-50 years, but make them the best of your life!

JILL ANGIE, AUTHOR, NOT YOUR AVERAGE RUNNER, HOST OF THE NOT YOUR AVERAGE RUNNER PODCAST

This is a creatively written collection of practical and fun tips to enhance and celebrate life after fifty. Suzy's engaging writing provides clues and evidence of what's possible when we finally put ourselves first. It's a must-read for any woman who seeks a deeper meaning and more joy in midlife and beyond!

CECA MIJATOVIC, FOUNDER AND COACH AT
TRUTH & DARE CANCER

Acknowledgements

. . . .

*"Mentors are all around us. Who makes you feel confident, inspired,
focused, and is willing to share their experience?"*
ANNA LETITIA COOK

I've been unbelievably fortunate to have and to have found the support, guidance, and mentorship that I've needed throughout my life.

I'm incredibly grateful for my family. My husband David is a loving rock of stability and is always supportive. My amazing kids, Max, Alex, and Zach are sensitive, talented, hilarious, and a joy to be with. You've all taught me how to celebrate life.

To my mom Wanda, sisters, and family back home. We've been through so much and we've thrived anyway. I love that you all also appreciate the importance of celebration. I hear your laughter in my mind all the time.

To my Uncle Bob Schneeweiss, thanks for teaching me so much about the art of celebration and for sharing idea #7 in this book.

I was so lucky to have my professional world open up to me after I turned 50. Special thanks and gratitude to my amazing coaching and business mentors Brooke Castillo, Susan Hyatt, Rachel Rodgers, Jenny Shih, and Kendrick Shope, who have taught me with such passion, creativity, and authenticity and shown me that having fun has to be part of the plan.

To Alex Franzen and Lindsey Smith. Thank you for launching a book writing course that grabbed my attention and encouraged me to believe that I had something important to share!

To the amazing "women in the middle" who are clients, listen to my podcast, and are members of my groups, I'm beyond grateful that the universe brought us together. Thank you for allowing me into your lives and trusting me to help you become the "Queen of Your Brain Domain," make the changes in your life you're excited about and believe that the best really is yet to come.

And finally, to my awesome girlfriends, thank you for being you. My life wouldn't be the same without you. Thanks for listening and always being there. Girlfriends make the world a better place.

Let's celebrate!

Introduction

....

Let's celebrate!

I mean, really. Let's look at this whole aging thing logically.
You're here.
You're alive.
That's reason enough to celebrate!

It's easy to get stuck in the muck and mire of midlife. And when you're stuck, you notice that something's changed. You wonder if it's a midlife crisis, but it doesn't feel THAT bad. You just feel a little off.

You might even feel a little weird about your age, maybe your job, and perhaps your kids becoming young adults. You may also be in the habit of only celebrating certain things but not life in general.

When you're stuck, it can be hard to find your way out of all of the stuckness. But it's possible.

That's what this little book is about. Unsticking yourself with a smile on your face.

You can absolutely get unstuck, but it won't happen by accident. When you shift your attention to how you can celebrate more, you're likely to also raise your awareness of what's truly possible at any age. There are other ways to think about things. You can also have more fun and be more intentional about celebrating.

I'm going to help you start moving in this direction.

Each chapter introduces you to one of six categories to help you celebrate your life after 50:
1. Celebrate your Age
2. Celebrate Self-Care
3. Celebrate your Passion
4. Celebrate your Relationships
5. Celebrate your Professional Self
6. Celebrate your Empty Nest

You'll get lots of amazing perspective in each chapter too.
- How I celebrated this topic
- Why it matters to celebrate
- Some interesting questions to ask yourself
- Thoughts about "the bottom line" on this topic
- Ideas for ways you can celebrate

By the end of the book, you'll have 50 ways to celebrate your life after 50 in six areas of your life. But there are some other key ingredients too. If you're curious enough, your path forward could also include:

- Laughter
- Insight
- Commitment
- And an open mind to create and allow more happiness.

I believe your life is a cause for celebration. You can believe this too. It all starts with your thinking!

Download the 50 Ways to Celebrate Life After 50 Tracker for motivation and inspiration! www.celebrate50.ca

1.

Celebrate Your Age
....

Do you celebrate your age? Are you someone who likes to celebrate birthdays? Or are you a little bit weird about aging these days? Aging is one of those topics that everyone feels differently about, that's for sure.

I definitely like to celebrate birthdays and getting older.

You see, getting older is something my parents didn't have that much of an opportunity to do. They died way too young.

As a midlife gal, I'm a lot older now than they ever were. Outliving your parents by decades isn't that common. This part of my life, however, is what shaped my attitude about aging being a cause for celebration.

The idyllic, sitcom-friendly life didn't happen for me. Far from it. Even now, decades later, I sometimes find myself thinking that I really find it hard to comprehend that all of this happened in my childhood and that THIS is my life.

But it did. And it is. And I thrived anyway.

I love my life. I've learned to accept the past as the past and live in the present.

Don't get me wrong, I had my share of difficulty and hardship, but I've been quite fortunate too. I grew up with a strong family structure and a rich family life including my amazingly strong stepmother, a few very loving aunts, three sets of grandparents, four sisters, a lot of St. Bernards, and an assortment of cats. There was plenty of laughter and lots of love.

And now, as a happily married, midlife mom, I'm extremely aware that I've outlived both of my parents and am way older than they ever were. I've been on this planet 25 years longer than my mother and 16 years longer than my father. Even though this fact is still sometimes hard for me to believe, I also feel incredibly grateful. And...I like to celebrate birthdays.

As a result of my personal history, I've always sensed that my life perspective was a little different than most. How could it not be?

I also think it was a main reason I've been open to mentors in my life. The universe provides mentors for you in all ages, shapes, and sizes. It's a beautiful thing the way this happens. I've been extremely fortunate and have had several men and women over the years become tremendous teachers and role models for me. I welcomed developing these relationships and learned so much. Thankfully, I was open to this kind of connection and have always been able to appreciate and celebrate it!

Finally, here's one of the biggest observations that has helped me celebrate life, even with this kind of adversity. You can actively choose how you want to think and feel about things you can't change. I've decided that I want to live a peaceful life full of excitement about what's possible.

I know that I can choose to feel this way because thoughts create feelings. I'm committed to understanding what thoughts I need to think to create feelings of gratitude and excitement. For example, the thought, "I know my parents loved me" creates a lot of gratitude. The thought, "there's still plenty of time to do amazing things" creates the feeling of excitement. Indeed, knowing and practicing this mindfulness skill is a cause for celebration!

Why It's Important to Celebrate Your Age:
What if aging was simply a reminder that you could be grateful that you're alive? That's it. No matter your age or milestone birthday, not everyone has the privilege to age. Not everyone can experience what you're doing right now...breathing, reading this book, enjoying nature, loving your family, petting your dog, listening to music, or watching the clouds.

It can be easy to lose sight of this when you get older, especially in midlife. Life can become overwhelming and difficult at times. It's common to start thinking that it's too late or too hard to make that change you're thinking about, or that the best really isn't yet to come. You might decide that you can't stand the way you look anymore with those unruly chin hairs or wrinkles between your brows. You might just think that you're too old now to do this or that.

Remember that these are just optional thoughts that you're thinking about what aging means to you. Notice how thinking about getting older like this makes you feel. My guess is, not that great. You don't have to think this way.

Ask Yourself This:

What if the best really is yet to come?

What if being your current age is an advantage that you just don't understand yet?

How are you not just older, but older, wiser and more fabulous than ever before?

_____

_____

_____

_____

_____

_____

_____

_____

_____

_____

What would it be like if you believed it was a privilege to age every year?

_____

_____

_____

_____

_____

_____

_____

_____

_____

_____

_____

_____

Why are you resistant to simply accepting the way your beautiful face is changing as it ages?

_____

_____

_____

_____

_____

_____

_____

_____

_____

_____

_____

_____

What feelings do you want to have in your life regularly? What do you need to think to create this for yourself?

_____

_____

_____

_____

_____

_____

_____

_____

_____

_____

The Bottom Line: You can think whatever you want about your age. Age is just a neutral number. If you want, you can always choose to think about that number in some way that's useful to you and makes you feel better instead of worse.

Always love to celebrate my birthday, 2015

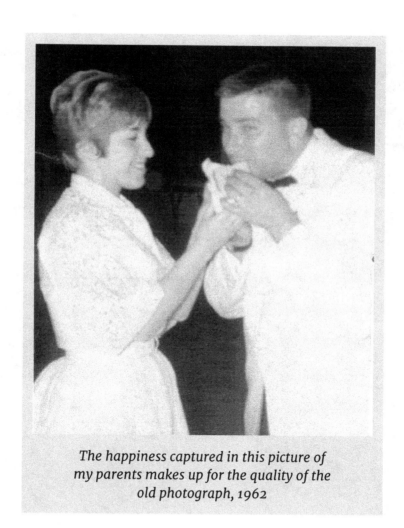

The happiness captured in this picture of my parents makes up for the quality of the old photograph, 1962

Things You Can Do To Celebrate Your Age

1. Celebrate your birthday by making a donation to your favorite cause.

2. Commit to experience joy on your own terms for the rest of your life.

3. Personally reach out to or even call your friends and family whose birthday reminders pop up on your Facebook feed, rather than only sending a message.

4. Question your thoughts about aging. Notice what you currently think about the age that you are. Then, ask yourself what you could make it mean on purpose instead.

5. Practice one new thought about what's possible in your life in the next year, five years, and ten years.

6. Create a daily gratitude habit. Have fun shopping for a gratitude journal...or several!

7. Pick the top 10 days you had last year and celebrate them by making a list and thanking the people you shared them with (this is a great New Year's Day or birthday activity).

8. Go out of your way to discover what else happened on the day you were born or the year of your birth (cards, horoscope, star chart, Life Magazine from that year, songs, playlist, etc.).

9. Google "success after 40" or "success after 50" and read about people who created successful magic later in life for inspiration. Write down what you want to apply to your own life.

2.

Celebrate Self-Care

·····························

It's easy to think you're too busy to take care of yourself. Even though you know that self-care is important, it's no surprise that it doesn't always become a priority. Do you know what it means and actively take steps to take care of yourself the way this term is intended?

Self-care is about providing care for yourself mentally, emotionally, and physically. So you can see, it's broader than the way you might commonly think of it, which might be more like doing small, occasional, "nice" things for yourself, like maybe finding time to have lunch with a friend or book a massage. These things are important, but they're not all that there is when it comes to self-care.

Self-care is intentional. It's you taking care of yourself to improve your overall well-being on purpose. Self-care also adds to your life and you're usually happier because of it. It's something that fuels you. It fills you up. It's also an area that many midlife women struggle to prioritize because it can feel indulgent. Notice what you might be thinking and feeling about it right now.

My story of self-care is about something I've always been good at prioritizing—having a creative hobby. It's definitely made me happier as a result. I love working with my hands.

There have been many hobbies like this over the years that I've been quite passionate about, including calligraphy, making FIMO jewelry and fondant cake flowers. But there's been one hobby in particular that illustrates the importance of self-care beautifully for me. I love beads. Specifically, I love making beaded wired head coverings for Jewish women. What I make is called a *kippah* and my version is unique, feminine and artsy; some women might choose to wear it to cover their hair at religious events like a prayer service, Jewish wedding or a *Bar* or *Bat Mitzvah*.

Now, I realize you may have never heard of such a thing, but it's popular in some circles and was in mine. When I started thinking about putting beads and wire together to make something like this, I was smitten. I couldn't stop thinking about all of the possibilities for creating these beautiful little functional art pieces for your hair.

I started making them like crazy. I looked online for my favorite beads which are abalone, pearls, and crystals. I searched for beads while on vacation too. I made dozens of them and eventually set up a little Etsy store.

This was just the outlet I needed and a great excuse to buy beads. When I make them, I get my space "all set up" just so, to really get in the creative zone. I always listen to the radio or a podcast, have a cup of tea, and completely lose myself for hours as I twist and weave the beads and wire into beautiful little creations. I love the way the abalone and crystals sparkle together. It satisfies my bead addiction. And, the customers who buy them are thrilled they've found such a special little *kippah*.

Then in May of 2017, about a decade or so into this little crafty adventure, something pretty shocking happened. My husband and I were walking the dog when I checked my phone and saw an unusual email. It was from the Museum of Modern Art (MoMA)! They contacted me through my Etsy site because they were interested in purchasing a *kippah* for an upcoming exhibit!

You should have seen my eyeballs when I read this email. I thought it was a hoax or spam or something.

My heart was pounding.

When I got back home, I quickly googled the exhibition and to my surprise and excitement, it was all real! The exhibit was called, Items: Is Fashion Modern?

The *kippah* was identified as one of the featured fashion-related items (clothing or accessories) that were impactful in the modern world for one reason or another. Mine was one of the 10 included in the *kippah* part of the exhibit and was also the only one made for women. As you can imagine, I was floored and honored.

It's one of the craziest, most delightful things that has ever happened to me. It's also something I could never have imagined. A picture of the *kippah* I made is also in the book about the exhibit. Thinking about it now still leaves me speechless.

I will never forget this once-in-a-lifetime experience and am so grateful.

This whirlwind of amazingness all came from doing something I really enjoyed. I had been lovingly making these little wearable art pieces for years. It was something that I always found time to do and was a hobby that was a reliable outlet for relaxation and creativity.

If you would have told me that something I made would be hanging in an exhibition at the Museum of Modern Art in 2017, there is absolutely no way I would have believed you.

I wouldn't have believed you if you told me this when I was a kid. I wouldn't have believed you if you told me this when I was an adult.

To be honest, if I hadn't seen it with my own eyes, I'm not sure I would have believed it at all. It was just too "big" to have been dreamed up as a possibility.

Yet, it happened. And it should be celebrated because just imagine what else might happen when you take care of yourself regularly and allow yourself to do and love what you love!

Ask Yourself This:

Why is it worth it for you to prioritize taking care of yourself?

_____

_____

_____

_____

_____

_____

_____

_____

_____

_____

_____

_____

What's the cost if you don't put yourself first?

_____

_____

_____

_____

_____

_____

_____

_____

_____

_____

_____

Why do you want to be the best person you can be?

_____

_____

_____

_____

_____

_____

_____

_____

_____

_____

_____

_____

Why does it feel indulgent to you to spend time and money on something you love?

_____

_____

_____

_____

_____

_____

_____

_____

_____

_____

_____

What will you be able to do better as a result of nurturing your soul?

_____

_____

_____

_____

_____

_____

_____

_____

_____

_____

_____

_____

_____

_____

_____

_____

_____

_____

_____

_____

_____

_____

The Bottom Line:

It's important to celebrate self-care because you owe it to yourself to maximize your midlife. If you don't take care of yourself, nobody will. These things don't just happen by accident. In order to take care of yourself mentally, emotionally and physically, you need to prioritize what you want to do and how you're going to do it. This will look different for everyone. You have to have your own back and make a real commitment to yourself or nothing will happen and years will fly by with you last on the list. Ask yourself if this is what you want.

Waiting patiently for MoMA to open, New York City, New York, 2017

← *A kippah and heart pendant that I made (Etsy, Wired Up Naturally), 2020*

→ *Wearing my kippah, 2020*

Things You Can Do To Celebrate Your Self-Care

10. Decide what putting yourself first means to you.

11. Make a commitment to put yourself first and think through how you're going to follow through.

12. Prioritize a way to move your body more. Commit to trying something new every year.

13. Answer this question: How can you make your body feel happier today?

14. Decide to get at least one hour more of sleep a night and drink one more glass of water a day.

15. Embrace a hobby. Elevate the experience in your life with new focus, equipment, space, or training.

16. Pick five places that you would regret not travelling to. Think about when and how you will make it happen.

17. Allow yourself to research and purchase the beauty product that you really want (shampoo, eye cream, special soap, mascara, etc.) and enjoy every last ounce.

18. Establish a morning and/or evening routine that really helps you ease into this part of the day.

3.

Celebrate Your Passion
....

Do you have a passion project...or something you can say, without a shadow of a doubt, IS your passion?

Passion feels bigger than a hobby. It's not just something you're excited about. It's something that is easy for you to go all in on with complete heart, mind, body, and soul. It's your mission on purpose. You can't imagine it not being part of your life. You choose to be involved, or not. Being involved is inspirational and enjoyable.

So many women our age aren't sure what they are passionate about. Isn't that curious?

Here's why I think this is.

First, I think that "women in the middle" like you aren't used to putting themselves first. You are quite comfortable, however, taking care of everyone else's needs way ahead of your own. And then before you know it, 20 years goes by and poof – you are out of practice.

In fact, it's likely that putting yourself first is so foreign to you that it feels uncomfortable, selfish or indulgent to actually focus on what you love, what you like, and what you want.

Second, I think that this whole passion thing seems elusive

because many "women in the middle" are trying too hard to find this magical, mystical thing that they wish they had in their lives.

Sometimes it's right under your nose and is based on something that has consistently brought you immense joy.

For me, it's whale watching.

It all started in 1985 in Kennebunkport, Maine.

I had always been attracted to the ocean and all things having to do with aquatic life. I was a little too fearful to take up scuba diving, but when I saw street signs to go whale watching, I couldn't believe what I was seeing. I had never heard anyone ever talking about this before. I couldn't stop thinking about going. I was obsessed and planned to go.

It was the most amazing day.

I saw a lot of fin whales and dolphins and I was hooked. I saw a dolphin jump clear out of the water—about six feet in the air—and actually got a picture of it in mid-air on my little pocket film camera. No rapid-fire back then.

I couldn't wait to do more of this. Thus, a true passion was born.

Over the years, I made sure to go whale watching as often as possible; I tried hard to plan vacations and road trips to coincide with whale migration. I learned everything I could about whales in my part of the world—the East Coast of the USA. The Cape Cod area became a favorite of mine because it was easily drivable and near family that I always wanted to visit. Perfect!

But, when I started earning an income after grad school, I started taking vacations to see whales in other places too.

First, I upgraded my camera because nature photography was also a passion. My first trip with my new camera was to Vancouver Island to see the orcas. That was my first zodiac boat trip too and it was amazing.

My next trip to see whales was a bigger one. In the early 90s, I discovered the gray whales in Baja California. I learned all about the gray whale migration, the longest migration of any mammal in the world.

This was before home internet was a thing. I ordered brochures and read everything I could. And that's when I discovered something called "a friendly encounter." Gray whales are curious about small boats and people and are known to come close to investigate. I couldn't wait to experience this for myself.

At this time, paying for this trip was a huge stretch. This trip meant going to a really remote camp in San Ignacio Lagoon for a few days, which was about half way up the coast of Baja, but on a little island.

I had never done anything like this and was new to adventure travel. But the possibility of having a friendly encounter had me giddy with excited anticipation.

I booked it. I enjoyed three full days of whale watching in a small wooden skiff, a boat that was about 20 feet long, with some other adventurous, whale loving souls.

All I can say is that it was a trip of a lifetime.

I saw dozens and dozens of gray whales and their brand new calves. And being on the water like that, I also saw all kinds of whale behaviours. Several whales came right over to our tiny boat. Some rubbed their barnacles and whale lice off on the bottom of the boat, gently spinning us around.

But nothing compared to coming eye to eye with one of the females. She was just massive (up to 49 feet long and 90,000 lbs or so) and so gorgeous. She was under the boat rubbing and then slowly rolled so that her eye was just about six inches under the water. I was leaning over the edge of the boat as she was looking at me and I was looking at her.

Our eyes were only about a foot apart. Her eye was huge, about the size of my head.

There we were...just looking at each other.

And then she blinked.

I don't know why it surprised me so much that she blinked. She was a mammal after all. But it did.

I was completely awestruck and immediately burst into tears as I felt so much emotion I could barely take it all in. It was clearly the most spiritually intense thing that's ever happened to me.

There was so much about that trip that was amazing. I loved it. And the reason I'm telling you about all of this is because this was the beginning of a passion.

It started out in a gentle way. I noticed a sign in Kennebunkport, Maine. I went on a whale watch. I was compelled to do more of them, to learn more, and to see more.

Eventually I purchased a good camera and whale watching became the most perfect combination of things that I loved doing: nature photography and whale heaven!

I grew to love photographing whales. The more I learned about whale behavior, the more I could anticipate it, and the better my pictures became.

I also loved being on the water.

I loved being outside with animals doing their thing.

I loved having a well-trained guide teaching while I was watching.

And now, I love sharing my love of whales with my family and learning more about whale conservation.

Whale watching became my passion.

I love finding ways to incorporate it into my life, especially when I can tag a whale watch on to a work-related trip.

I love the way I feel when I spend time doing it, even if it's only for a few hours every year or two.

I've been whale watching dozens of times and can't wait to go again. It's my happy place.

In fact, you will not be surprised when you see me organizing a retreat some day soon that combines whale watching with my other love, coaching amazing midlife women! Talk about a great way to take a deep dive! Stay tuned and make sure to contact me if you would be interested in this kind of an experience!

Ask Yourself This:

If you won the lottery, what's the first thing that pops into your mind that you would do? This is often a clue to your passion.

_____

_____

_____

_____

_____

_____

_____

_____

_____

_____

_____

_____

What is the one thing that has consistently brought you joy throughout your life? There's likely something about this that can help you determine your passion.

_____

_____

_____

_____

_____

_____

_____

_____

_____

_____

_____

What makes you tick? What's something that really excites you, that you always want to learn more about or get more involved in?

_____

_____

_____

_____

_____

_____

_____

_____

_____

_____

_____

_____

Why don't you have more of this passion in your life? See if you like your reason or not.

_____

_____

_____

_____

_____

_____

_____

_____

_____

_____

The Bottom Line:
Your passion can add depth and joy to your life. It's like an extra-meaningful sparkle. Passion gives you purpose. It can help you set fulfilling goals. You can also inspire and share with other like-minded people. Having a passion will introduce you to new experiences and people throughout your life. Living like this is a beautiful way to put yourself first and have more fun.

Watching a gray whale and her calf, San Ignacio Lagoon, Baja California Sur, Mexico 1992

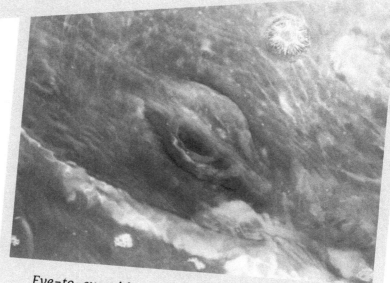

Eye-to-eye with a gray whale, San Ignacio Lagoon, Baja California Sur, Mexico, 1992

Things You Can Do To Celebrate Your Passion

19 Focus on your passion. Identify it. Embrace it!

20 Spend resources on your passion. Give yourself a time and money budget and enjoy the spend.

21 Explore ways to deepen your passion and enjoyment of it. Think more broadly about what else you can do with it.

22 Share your passion with friends and family. Invite them in. Teach them.

23 Be curious when you see other passionate people in action. Watch documentaries. Follow-up.

24 Take your passion on the road. Experience it in other cities, other countries, and with other people.

25 Support other passions. Being in passionate communities feels great and is really inspirational!

26 Continue to learn and grow with your passion. Take the course. Talk to the speaker. Join the club. Spend time with experts.

4.

Celebrate Your Relationships

Relationships are an interesting part of your life that are often not as intentional as they could be. It's typically a common area of regret too, as you age. I think relationships should also be a cause for celebration and something to amplify!

My story is about a specific type of relationship, that is, a long-term friendship. I made my 50th birthday even better when I celebrated with my amazing friend from high school, Karen.

I started to think about how I wanted to celebrate my 50th birthday a few months before the big day. I didn't have to think that hard actually. I knew I wanted to spend time with my best friend from childhood, spend time near the ocean and eat seafood. With this clarity, the plan was pretty much hatched and it wasn't too hard to sell my bestie on the idea. She turned 50 the year before so it was a double celebration.

I booked our timeshare in Punta Gorda, Florida. We had a two bedroom suite on the water with the most adorable, perfect balcony with a view of the harbor. We shopped, collected shells, went to a wildlife center, visited the Ringling Museum, saw manatees, and made beaded jewelry. Heaven!

We also enjoyed sitting on the little balcony overlooking the harbor watching boats while sipping wine and enjoying little appetizers.

One time, we did a little visioning type of exercise in special journals that I purchased for the trip. Each of us came up with 10 things we wanted to prioritize going forward in our life.

This exercise woke me up a bit on several topics. One of the most powerful realizations was that we wanted to make sure that we saw each other at least once a year. That may not seem that earth shattering, but we were kind of winging it with our visits. She lived in Florida and I'm in Ontario, about 1400 miles apart. We need to be more intentional about it and not accidentally let a few years go by between visits.

We made a commitment to each other that visits would be more consistent from now on and we've held to our word. I'm also particularly proud of myself that I figured out how to incorporate her skills as a yoga teacher into my work as a midlife coach. She is the guest yoga instructor at my online and in-person retreats! How's that for being intentional!

Ask Yourself This:

Do you initiate socializing with your friends? If not, why not? Do you have enough friends? What can you do to make more friends at this time in your life?

_____

_____

_____

_____

_____

_____

_____

_____

_____

_____

_____

_____

How can you get more involved and connect with your community?

_____

_____

_____

_____

_____

_____

What can you do to express your feelings more to those you care about?

_____

_____

_____

_____

_____

_____

What might you regret if you don't become more intentional with your relationships?

_____

_____

_____

_____

_____

_____

_____

_____

_____

_____

_____

Are there experiences you always imagined you would have with your family or friends that you haven't had yet? If so, what's your plan?

_____

_____

_____

_____

_____

_____

_____

_____

_____

The Bottom Line:

It's quite common to regret losing touch with friends in midlife. It's an important area of your life to be intentional about. Being social, connecting and having friends can have positive effects on mental health, stress reduction and overall well-being. In general, friends can be a reliable source of fun and can even be good for your health!

Beautiful view from our balcony, Punta Gorda, Florida, 2013

At my silly best with Karen, Punta Gorda, Florida, 2013

Things You Can Do To Celebrate Your Relationships

27 Pick three ways you can be more intentional with important relationships.

28 Up your communication habit. Actually write letters to people and send them.

29 Make sure to express your feelings to your friends more than you do.

30 Prioritize conversations over brevity with texts. Call three people this month instead.

31 Notice when you feel too rushed to listen and commit to change this habit.

32 Think about the most meaningful times you've shared with those you love and consider repeating them.

33 Take turns planning some fun with your favorite people on purpose.

34 Identify one thing you really want to experience with someone close to you. Plan to do it.

5.

Celebrate Your Professional Self
....

Are you clear about all the ways you make a formal or professional contribution? I like thinking about work this way because your professional contribution can go beyond how you earn an income. For example, you're often a professional in the way that you volunteer as well. Think about celebrating your professional self in this context.

How excited are you these days at work? Are you feeling bored and stuck? Career malaise is something that so many midlife women experience.

One reason is that your job may have gotten stagnant with fewer challenges lately. Another reason might be that your values have changed. You may start thinking that there must be more out there for you. You're just not fulfilled or reaching your potential anymore.

That's what happened to me. I studied psychology in university and got an MA in Applied Social Psychology. My emphasis back then was on qualitative methodology, ethnographic research, and program evaluation. Overall, I enjoyed my 27 year career in health education and health promotion, where my skills and training were applied and quite relevant. I loved my work for most of my career and felt creative and proud of the way I was able to contribute in this field.

During the last five years of my job, however, I started to feel differently. I noticed that I just wasn't feeling content anymore, which was totally different from the way I had ever felt in my career. I was bored and craved more growth and challenge. I also figured out that I really wanted to work more directly with the people I was helping. I slowly realized that there was nothing wrong with my job. But there WAS something wrong with me IN my job.

I had been there too long.

I was pretty shocked one morning when I got a weird sounding knock at my office door. I was told I was needed for a meeting... and then the harsh reality of being laid off set in. Even though I fantasized about this for years, I felt sucker-punched and betrayed when it actually happened to me.

My heart was beating so loudly. I was overwhelmed by all the people in the room waiting for me. I was assured my lay off had had nothing to do with my performance. Receiving that news was a beautiful gift because when you're in that situation, you don't know what's going on and can easily think the worst, which, of course, I did.

There was something familiar about the room for the meeting.

I couldn't help but notice where the meeting was. This was the exact room where my job interview took place almost two decades earlier...to the date.

This felt poetic to me somehow, like this chapter was complete.

As I took what felt like a walk of shame down the long hallway back to my office, my colleagues greeted me at my office door with a lot of shock and concern.

It was a crazy, stressful day. Before long, however, getting laid off felt more and more like the gift that I was too afraid to give myself. The truth is that I wanted to leave, but couldn't get over how indulgent it felt to leave without a clear plan. I was stuck and unhappy for five years though and now, I had help making the change I knew I really wanted.

It took about six months for me to start to figure out what I wanted to do next. I realized that a big part of what had been missing for me in my career was working closely with people. I also realized that I craved becoming an entrepreneur. Somewhere along the line, I discovered life coaching. I was curious and inspired. I felt drawn toward it.

I trained to be a Master Certified Life Coach at The Life Coach School. I loved coaching clients and also had the opportunity to teach. Becoming an entrepreneur was so creative and exciting. I felt more motivated, focused and engaged in growth than I had in years!

At first, I thought about my professional life as having two distinct phases: my first career in health education and then my second career as a life coach. I thought about them as though they were separate parts of my professional life.

Upon reflection though, I see things differently now. I believe that the professional journey is not always completely understood and is a cause for celebration. What I mean by that is I was always on the path that brought me where I am now. The path was preparing me. Everything I had done contributed to where I ended up. Even though I felt like I was lost, I was finding my way.

My journey started much earlier than I thought. What I chose to study in university, the in-depth interviewing skills I acquired in grad school, my passion for being in a cause-oriented profession and being attracted to being an entrepreneur most of my life all helped me get where I am today. It's so fun to think back to my first entrepreneurial experience when I was 13 years old with calligraphy and doing invitation envelopes! I see now that I was always on the right path.

I love knowing this about my life. Instead of being hard on myself about wasting time and being stuck for so long, I've learned to honor and celebrate my ability to trust myself and keep moving forward.

Ask Yourself This:

What kind of professional contribution is important to you and why?

How do you want to feel when you're at work?

Does change scare you? If so, why?

_____

_____

_____

_____

_____

_____

_____

_____

_____

_____

_____

_____

How do you want to grow as a professional? Are you doing this?

_____

_____

_____

_____

_____

_____

_____

_____

_____

_____

_____

What has always been consistent for you in terms of what you're attracted to professionally? What can you learn from this?

_____

_____

_____

_____

_____

_____

_____

_____

_____

_____

_____

What do you believe about the possibility that you're just now entering the most creative and inspirational time of your career?

_____

_____

_____

_____

_____

_____

_____

_____

_____

The Bottom Line:

By the time you're in midlife, you've spent a couple of decades honing your skills and have had a plethora of rich experiences. Maybe you have a career; maybe you've been a professional volunteer. You've been putting yourself out there and making a contribution for a long time. When you look closely, you'll no doubt see that the path you've been on makes sense in your life. Trust yourself. Your professional self deserves to be celebrated.

Women in the Middle Podcast: Loving Life after 50

← Enjoying the view, Coaching Retreat, Toronto, Ontario, 2019

→ Enjoying the giraffes, Coaching Retreat, The Living Desert Zoo and Gardens, Palm Desert, California, 2020

Things You Can Do To Celebrate Your Professional Self

35 Practice feeling proud; collect and perhaps even display your diplomas and certifications (put them in a binder or in a frame).

36 Spend time on LinkedIn and stay current, even if you're not looking for a job.

37 Think about what you want to be known for and make changes in your LinkedIn profile to reflect it.

38 Continue to network, even when you're not "looking" for a job; it helps you in so many ways. Aim to connect with at least one new person professionally each month.

39 Think about what you can learn from your thoughts about what you wanted to be when you grew up.

40 Identify three professional things you did that you are really proud of and what you can learn from them.

41 Be a mentor to someone younger.

42 Think about what else you want to accomplish and/ or experience professionally and allow yourself to dream big!

6.

Celebrate Your Empty Nest
....

The whole empty nest thing can be jarring. It seems like it's one of those secrets that nobody really tells you about. There doesn't seem like there's a lot of prep, even though there's usually been about 18 years or so.

The empty nest transition was surprising for me. I had three kids in 3.5 years. They are close in age and each two years apart in school. This was relevant to the way the empty nest transition rolled out.

When my oldest went away to school, it reminded me of the first time he went down a steep ski hill with an instructor. I was definitely scared and excited for him at the same time. Fast forward about 10 years to the night before he moved out for university; I felt panicky about whether or not I had taught him everything he needed to know.

I didn't anticipate the effect on the two brothers still at home. The dynamic of everything changed. And then, one by one, each of them moved out to go to school. And then there were none at home. And it got quiet and pretty boring.

Little did we realize how much we relied on the kids for entertainment. The kids are loud and funny. They have great friends, who are also loud and funny, and this all made for a busy and welcoming family life. We felt a noticeable difference with a quiet "empty" home.

We filled part of the hole left by the kids with an adorable empty nest dog, Niko the Newf. He's an extremely handsome 120 lb. Landseer Newfoundland. Big. Fluffy. Slobbery. Keeps us busy. Slowly but surely, we found our identities again. They weren't very far away, but definitely needed to be rediscovered.

And, we also found cause for celebration.

We love visiting our guys in their student apartments and also loved when they came home. The house lights up immediately. So does Niko. He gets so excited when his "brothers" come back.

But you know what else happened? We also started to get more comfortable shifting to being empty nest parents of adult children who needed us less.

We grew to appreciate the quiet.

There was far less cooking.

And life became less complicated overall, with little planning, coordination and car jockeying.

Oh yeah, exceptionally fun winter vacation plans made more sense as a sure-fire time to have a family get-together.

It became a simpler life with more freedom.

It seems like the reality is that the kids move back and forth and in and out depending on their education and job situations. And we're fine with that.

They still need us but not in the same way. They love coming home but love their independent lives more. They seem to appreciate everyone's strengths and weaknesses with less annoyance and more humor. They also love and rely on each other as brothers. All of this is a cause for celebration.

My empty nest dog, Niko the Newf,
Kawartha Lakes, Ontario, 2014

Ask Yourself This:

What kind of relationship do you want to have with your adult kids?

_____

_____

_____

_____

_____

_____

_____

_____

_____

_____

_____

Who do you want to be now that you have more time to yourself
and why?

_____

_____

_____

_____

_____

_____

_____

_____

_____

_____

_____

_____

What did you love about raising your family? How might you be able to enjoy that sort of thing with an older family?

_____

_____

_____

_____

_____

_____

_____

_____

_____

_____

_____

What are the top three things that you want to do most, now that you can?

_____

_____

_____

_____

_____

_____

_____

_____

_____

_____

_____

_____

_____

_____

_____

_____

_____

_____

_____

_____

_____

_____

The Bottom Line:

Having kids who are ready to move out and learn how to become independent is a beautiful thing. It's something you can be proud of. It's a time to celebrate your opportunity as well, as your world opens up to all kinds of things that are possible for you with the increased energy and focus available. You could decide to think that...it's party time!

Things You Can Do To Celebrate Your Empty Nest

43 Claim some of the newly available space in your house for yourself.

44 Regret-proof your family experiences and vacations by thinking carefully about what is a priority, even now with older kids.

45 Have fun writing letters to your kids and mail them, the old fashioned way.

46 Be intentional about the kind of relationship you want to have with your young adult(s). What can you do to create this?

47 Consider sharing your life with an empty nest dog... or two.

48 Handwrite your favorite recipes and share them with your kids.

49 Allow yourself to ditch the guilt about ordering in and elevate the dining experience in your home with full place settings, music, and a relaxed atmosphere. You don't always have to cook it yourself to make dinner happen.

50 Establish fun new family traditions, both with the grown up kids and without them. Being silly and having a great time is always a good thing, no matter your age!

Time to Celebrate!
If Not Now, When?
....

As you can see, there are many ways to think about what's worthy of a celebration. I hope that offering thought-provoking questions and suggestions for new ways to think about these six areas of your life and interesting ways to celebrate them create motivation and inspiration for you to have more fun and be more grateful about this time in your life.

If you're in a midlife funk and feel stuck, remember that it's totally common. You can actually unstick yourself because being stuck is based on the way you're thinking.

You have more choices than you're likely aware of about the way you think about some of these types of midlife-related things. The first step is increasing your awareness of what you're thinking. Adopting a new mindset that includes more excitement about acknowledging what's important, memorable, and meaningful to you can really add a lot to celebrating your life overall.

You can start with the 50 ways to celebrate your life after 50 outlined in this book. I'm sure that before you know it, your creativity will be primed and you'll be more inspired than you've been in ages to come up with even more ideas of your own.

Celebrating MORE is fun! You can learn to be more intentional about increasing the celebration factor in your life.

Actually...celebrating more is a choice you can make right now. Midlife is the perfect time to do it.

You'll have to change your mindset about what's celebration-worthy, and you'll have to practice pumping up your celebration muscle, but I have a feeling you're up for it. You'll never look back.

Just focus on one thought and one celebration at a time!

Download the 50 Ways to Celebrate Life After 50 Tracker for motivation and inspiration! www.celebrate50.ca

About The Author
....

Suzy Rosenstein, MA wants to live in a world where aging is cool and thinking about possibility is fun. As a master certified life coach, midlife mentor, and entrepreneur, she's more creative, having more fun and more fulfilled than ever before.

She's been able to help hundreds of women get unstuck and get excited about their lives again through private and group coaching and her new midlife membership, The Finally First Club, as well as her popular podcast, Women in the Middle: Loving Life after 50. Listeners and clients praise her for being refreshingly upbeat in the way she coaches on the ups and downs of midlife with wisdom and humor.

When she's not coaching, Suzy can be found hanging with her family, playing with her big, slobbery dog, talking to her chatty parrot, taking pictures or watching whales. She lives in Ontario, Canada. To learn more, visit her website: Suzyrosenstein.com

CPSIA information can be obtained
at www.ICGtesting.com
Printed in the USA
LVHW050543300121
677807LV00004B/512